TOY SOLDIERS

THE COLLECTOR'S CORNER

TOY SOLDIERS

Grange
BOOKS

A Quantum Book

Published by Grange Books
an imprint of Grange Books Plc
The Grange
Kingsnorth Industrial Estate
Hoo, nr Rochester
Kent ME3 9ND

ISBN 1 84013 257 4

This book is produced by
Quantum Books Ltd
6 Blundell Street
London N7 9BH

Project Manager: Rebecca Kingsley
Art Director: Siân Keogh
Project Editor: Jo Wells
Designer: Martin Laurie
Editor: Linda Doeser
Assistant Designer: Ben Cumming

The material in this publication previously appeared in *Toy Soldiers* and *Tin Toys*

QUMCCTS
Set in Gill Sans
Reproduced in Singapore by Eray Scan Pte Ltd
Printed in Singapore by Star Standard Industries (Pte) Ltd

CONTENTS

The Long History of Toy Soldiers 6

From Toy to Valuable Collectable 11

Solid, Connoisseur and
Hollow-cast Models 17

Composition and
Slush-cast Figures 33

The Plastic Battleground 39

Aluminium, Paper and
Wood Figures 47

A New Era –
Toy Soldiers Since 1973 49

Souvenirs and Memorabilia 63

THE LONG HISTORY OF
TOY SOLDIERS

• • • •

BELOW Austrian flat figures (circa 1930) of American War of Independence troops.

Miniature soldiers can be traced to Ancient Egypt. Small warrior-like figures were found in the tombs of the Pharaohs. Solid figures from Roman times (thought to have been toys) can be seen in the British Museum and in Xian, China, a life-size terracotta army was discovered. Such was, and is, the passion for military history. Some of the first commercially-manufactured toy soldiers were made of lead in Nuremberg in the mid-eighteenth century.

At first, toy soldiers were expensive and tended to be bought for the children of the nobility. But as the manufacturing process became increasingly sophisticated and less labour-intensive, more and more cheaper tin soldiers became available. By the late nineteenth century, boxes of toy soldiers were a common sight under Victorian Christmas trees.

Bright young men in gorgeous uniforms, well-fed and groomed horses, fairy-tale forts and

RIGHT Hollow-cast (circa 1920) British Army infantryman in an unusually casual pose. It stands 65mm (2¹/₂in) high.

immaculate army vehicles – all present a picture of military life that was very far from the reality of war. When a boy played with toy soldiers, army life must have seemed exciting and romantic – soldiers dressed in splendid uniforms to perform deeds of valour.

Toy soldier 'flats'

Metal was by far the best material for representing 'men in action', as the figures could be moulded in detail and given a base on which to stand.

In the 'flat' method of production, two-part moulds were made from slate, stone, wood or bronze. The general detail of the figure was gouged out and then the fine detail carefully incised with etching tools.

A pouring channel was cut out and pegs linked the two sides of the mould together. Then the manufacturer's secret

LEFT Solid miniature (1970) of an officer from the Zulu War by Tradition of London. Highly-detailed, it stands 54mm (2¹/₄in) high.

recipe of molten metal (a mixture of tin, lead, antimony and bismuth) was poured into the pre-heated mould.

Collectable 'flats' are today valued according to the quality of the engraved detail, the verve of the outline and the skill of the painter. The first great makers of tin 'flats' were the Hilpert family (1720–1822), best known for a series of finely detailed monkeys and classical figures. Their regiments of soldiers were exported as far afield as the United States and are regarded as the aristocrats of the genre.

German production of tin 'flats' reached its peak in the mid-nineteenth century, though there were small factories in Great Britain, Denmark, France, Switzerland and the United States. The Napoleonic Wars inspired a spate of table-top battles in Europe and the toy manufacturers turned out soldiers by the thousand.

ABOVE A mixture of Comet and Authenticast solid figures, 54mm (2¹/₄in) tall.

The most prolific of the German makers was Ernst Heinrichsen who, from about 1850, concentrated on a 30mm (1¼in) size. This is now accepted as the 'Nuremberg Scale'. Heinrichsen depicted battles from all periods, including classical antiquity, the Crusades and the Crimean War. Ernst Wilhelm was the last of the Heinrichsen family and died in 1938.

Apart from the famous Hilperts and Heinrichsens, there were many other makers of 'flats' based in Berlin, Gotha, Luneberg, Diessen and Potsdam. Unfortunately, the soldiers are not marked and even the boxes rarely carry the manufacturer's name. The soldiers were originally sold

by weight rather than number and the smallest box was the 113gm (4oz) size. Some of the large, boxed gift sets of figures for a complete battle were sold with maps.

One German firm still producing 'flats' is Babette Schweitzer, a concern that creates both decorative and toy items for export all over the world. Other smaller makers produce soldiers and scenes in limited numbers for the collectors' market. There is also some production of unpainted figures.

The hollow-cast method

The invention of the hollow-cast lead soldier, devised in the United Kingdom by William Britain Junior in 1893,

ABOVE A 54mm (2¼in) pre-'dimestore' American infantry figure (circa 1950) by Lincoln Logs.

LEFT Victorian-style sailor (circa 1920) from the American Soldier Company.

ABOVE This 60mm (2³/₈in) nurse in cape figure was made by Alymer of Spain. Alymer is best-known for its historical and personality figures series and heraldic knights.

LEFT This 75mm (3in) high figure is made of a composition material including wood flour. Made by Playwood Plastics in 1942, it kept toy soldier production going during lead shortages.

LEFT Made by Deetail in 1979, it is cowboy and Mexican versus American Indians around a Herald totem pole.

started the toy soldier revolution, and continental toy soldiers soon fell from favour with the patriotic British consumer. Many companies imitated this production process.

Production continued in Europe up to and during the First World War, with minor attempts being made to produce toy soldiers in the United States. By the Second World War, the American market was self-sufficient with ranges of slush- or hollow-cast soldiers.

Most production stopped during the Second World War; up to this time Germany, France and Italy had continued to issue solid toy soldiers, while British manufacturers continued with the more economical method of hollow-casting.

During the 1930s, Germany had started producing composition figures made of a mixture of sawdust, pumice power and glue, sculptured around a wire frame or armature. After the Second World War, the production of lead figures resumed, but experiments were taking place with plastic, and by the early 1950s, many United Kingdom and continental companies were turning to the plastic injection moulding system.

The manufacture of hollow-cast lead figures in the United Kingdom ceased in 1966 when legislation prohibited the sale of items that contained lead paint. Military miniatures of a 'non-toxic' material (lead figures coated with lead-free paint) filled the gap between 1966 and 1972, when white metal New Toy Soldiers were devised.

Soldiers as collectables

In common with all fields of collecting, it is when items become difficult to come by that the desire to accumulate increases. So it is with toy soldiers. Collecting started to become fashionable in the 1960s as the hollow-cast and other lead soldiers were discontinued. Toy soldiers made of metal, though, are still the most avidly collected.

Throughout their history, model soldiers have appealed to adults as well as children and expensive versions in precious metals and precise detail have been made alongside cheap, mass-produced examples. Because so many figures have survived in good condition, soldiers form one of the most active collecting areas, with their own specialist groups: those who collect antique figures in near-perfect condition for display and those who use the models for war games.

As the value of soldiers in original condition has increased, collectors treat their acquisitions with great respect, and repairing and re-modelling work has decreased. The importance of original packaging is also respected, as the additional value of a boxed set is generally recognized. It was once quite common for collectors to remove sets and discard the boxes. As in all areas of soldier collecting, boxed sets are preferred; those containing 'flats' are especially prized, because they are decorated with the medals won at various exhibitions.

The greatest amount of work was lavished on large, doll-like figures that can stand up to 30cm (12in) high. Soldiers of this type, often dressed in fabrics from actual uniforms, have been made since the sixteenth century, though the majority that appear on the market were made after 1800. In general, this is a neglected area of soldier-collecting, despite the fact that the toys – sometimes complete with swords, guns and equipment – are fascinating historical documents.

RIGHT Barclay's 75mm (3in) 'dimestore' infantryman with removable tin helmet.

RIGHT Solid-cast and detailed Greenwood and Ball Highland officer.

FROM TOY TO
VALUABLE COLLECTABLE

● ● ● ●

The reasons why people collect toy soldiers are many and varied. Many older people collect soldiers for nostalgic reasons, wanting reminders of childhood toys that have long since disappeared; other people have a fascination for a particular type of soldier; for others it may be an extension of a general interest in all things military; still others may enjoy collecting so that they can build up and manoeuvre entire armies in mock battles; and, of course, some people see collecting tin soldiers as a financial investment. However, this latter reason is rarely the primary one.

Collecting metal toy soldiers became fashionable in the early 1960s. As ranges and lines were discontinued, so

BELOW An imaginative, hand-painted white lead set by Dorset Soldiers.

collectors began to acquire them, realizing that they would no longer be available through the usual retail outlets. Since then, the hobby has grown and developed to embrace more and more people.

Specializing your collection

What kind of soldiers you decide to collect is very much a matter of personal preference. However, there are some general factors that are useful to bear in mind before you get started because they will help you to decide in what direction you would like your collection to go.

The first question to ask yourself is what you are particularly interested in. Perhaps you will want to collect a particular type of soldier, or you may have an interest in the work of a particular manufacturer or the soldiers from one country or even from a certain period.

Collections can be arranged in several different ways: by manufacturer, size, type of material or you can concentrate on certain periods in history, individual wars and campaigns, types of uniform or even particular regiments. It may be that your collection will start as a mixture of items and then become specialized as you become more involved.

ABOVE Minikins 1950 souvenir for Fort William Henry in Canada.

RIGHT, TOP AND BOTTOM Plastic figures made in Hong Kong in the 1970s for the British market.

Another factor to bear in mind is cost. Some soldiers are much more expensive than others and you need to be able to assess which areas of collecting will suit your pocket, as well as your taste. If you are intent on putting together an entire army or simply want to amass a huge collection, bear in mind the financial investment that will be required.

It is useful to scout around the various toy soldier outlets and talk to other collectors if you are a newcomer to the hobby. This will give you an idea of what is available and at what price.

Where to buy

Collecting toy soldiers has never been easier than it is currently. As the hobby

has grown, specialist shops have sprung up and you will find one in most of the world's major cities.

In addition to these shops, soldiers are commonly available from toy shows, flea markets, antiques fairs and markets, and at auctions. Then there is always the chance that you will find something special at a car boot sale, jumble sale or in a junk shop. Swapmeets are also popular, where you can meet with other enthusiasts and swap items and information.

Going, going, gone!

Auctions are a good source of toy soldiers, but they can be daunting. Attending auctions can be both a source of revenue (if you are selling) and an opportunity to purchase toy soldiers either as single pieces or in multiple lots. They also provide an opportunity to see what is on the market and to get an idea of what the prices are. There are several basic rules that will make the purchase of toy soldiers more enjoyable.

1. Make yourself aware of each individual auction house's rules, commission rate and VAT or sales tax.

2. Remember that the 'hammer price' will, in most cases, be subject to a basic percentage rate of auctioneer's commission and in some cases, usually indicated in the catalogue, a VAT or sales tax charge.

3. Obtain an auction catalogue in advance and view the items you wish to purchase.

4. If you are selling at auction, take into account the auction house commission rules, as this amount will be deducted from the price that your items eventually realize.

5. Consult the auction house regarding reserve prices for your items in order to ensure that if your property does not reach the expected price level, it will not be sold for less than your agreed reserve.

RIGHT A rare example of a French hollow-cast figure of a Tommy throwing a grenade.

There were many French manufacturers of hollow-cast figures. Mignot, better known for its solid items, made some hollow-cast soldiers. The bases of some of the French hollow-cast soldiers are marked with various initials, including LP and GM, but these firms defy identification even today.

Items found in their original boxes provide obvious evidence of the manufacturer. If you can get hold of original or reproduction catalogues, they will help with identification, as will any of the specialist books dealing with identification..

Identification

The majority of toy soldiers bear some kind of mark on the underside of the base. Sometimes this shows the country where the soldier was manufactured, but it can also include the name of the manufacturer. Some pieces are marked in such a way as to indicate their origins.

John Hill and Co. marked 'Johillo' or 'John Hill' on their figures, but also stamped them with an abbreviation of 'copyright', spelled 'copyrt'.

Britains Ltd. marked nearly every figure, but used a variety of marks, including their name, Britains Ltd. Only very early examples may not carry a mark. For a while, the company used paper labels until all their moulds could be retooled to accommodate the copyright stamp. These paper labels are not always extant.

Soldiers on parade

Part of the pleasure of having a collection of toy soldiers is being able to enjoy looking at them. The most popular method of displaying soldiers is in cases or on shelves. It helps if these are enclosed so that dust does not become a problem, because soldiers can be fiddly and time-consuming to clean. However, air should be allowed to circulate round the items.

It is up to the collector to decide which soldiers he wants to display together.

RIGHT French Mameluke in turban, 54mm (2¹/₄in) high and hollow-cast.

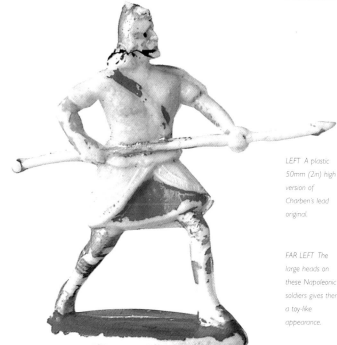

LEFT A plastic 50mm (2in) high version of Charben's lead original.

FAR LEFT The large heads on these Napoleonic soldiers gives them a toy-like appearance.

You may make the selection according to size, regiments and so on. Particularly interesting or attractive soldiers can be displayed singly. Some collectors prefer to arrange their figures to form a scene or diorama, perhaps depicting a real or imaginary reconstruction of a state occasion, battle or historical incident.

Storage and care

Those unable to display their collections should ensure that lead soldiers are stored in a dry and well-ventilated area in strong cardboard boxes with a light covering of tissue paper. Plastic figures tend to become brittle and they should be stored in only a single row, not stacked row upon row.

A cautionary word needs to be said about the problem of lead rot, sometimes called lead disease, which can attack lead toy soldiers, causing a great deal of damage and deterioration. The signs to watch out for are a grey powdering of the lead. When lead rot is spotted, immediately isolate the affected item in order to prevent other pieces being affected.

Although much research has been carried out into the causes of this problem, without any conclusive results, it is known that storage in damp conditions does not help. And it has also been proved that direct contact with oak wood can be a contributory factor to the onset of the disease. As a general rule, display or storage in airtight conditions is to be avoided.

Repair and restoration

It is not necessary to look out exclusively for tin soldiers in good condition. Repainting, converting, repairing and restoring toy soldiers for your own pleasure is a worthwhile and satisfying creative exercise. A growing number of collectors are trying to obtain broken or damaged toy soldiers because they have developed a special interest in repairing old toy soldiers, taking pleasure in restoring them to their former glory. Other people obtain broken or even complete toy soldiers and convert them into something else. They may put together pieces from two or more incomplete soldiers to make a whole one.

Value and condition

If a figure is in good condition when you buy it and remains so, the likelihood is that it will retain or increase its value. Repainting, converting and repairing tend to devalue figures.

For those who are interested in investment, it is a very good idea to keep an inventory of your collection. Make a note of the price you paid originally for each item and from time to time find out from toy soldier dealers what your collection is currently worth. This running record is interesting for its own sake and is useful for insurance purposes.

RIGHT This plastic casting of a mounted Roman legionnaire was made by Hausser (circa 1960–70). It is 100mm (4in) high and the rider is detachable.

CHAPTER TWO

SOLID, CONNOISSEUR AND HOLLOW-CAST MODELS

• • • •

Solid toy soldiers were first produced as a commercial venture in about 1760. At first they were flat, but the desire for more realistic figures took hold and the French firm Lucotte produced solid, fully-rounded toy soldiers depicting units of the French Imperial Army. These were the first toy soldiers representing the real thing. During the Napoleonic Wars, Lucotte issued a range of troops from the conflicts.

Lucotte solid-cast soldiers

Lucotte toy soldiers may be easily identified by the Imperial bee, which is stamped on the underside of the base of each figure. Lucotte toy soldiers are rare today, but a mirrored display case at Blenheim Palace in Oxfordshire, England contains a unique array of Napoleonic troops by Lucotte.

The solid method of manufacture involved a two-piece mould that was filled with molten lead. After the lead had cooled, the figure was extracted. The continental manufacturers produced heads from separate moulds that were then plugged into the body of the figure.

By 1825 CBG Mignot of Paris had taken over the firm of Lucotte, and began to introduce many new ranges of toy soldiers. It produced almost all of the French and French-Colonial regiments together with representative figures from many of the world's other armies, particularly those in conflict with the French. They were hand-painted and fairly accurate in uniform detail. Mignot was in existence until the early 1990s.

LEFT These 30mm (1¼in) high, lead 'flats' (circa 1920s) were available in cigarette packets.

Heyde of Dresden

Germany runs a close second to France in the production of solid-cast toy soldiers. Georg Heyde of Dresden produced toy soldiers from 1870 to 1944, when the factory was destroyed by Allied bombing raids. Heyde figures come in a range of sizes, but most are 45mm (1¾in) in size, unlike the 54mm (2¼in) figures of Lucotte and Mignot, which has become the standard and recognized size of a toy soldier. Toy soldiers are measured from the top of the base to the forehead, which means that thick bases or tall headgear do not affect the scale.

BELOW A rare 200mm (8in) high, Heyde-made British lancer (circa 1920s).

Like Mignot figures, Heyde toy soldiers have plug-in heads, which means that a whole variety of regiments could be created by putting different heads on different torsos. The Heyde range also featured some massive display sets. These included soldiers in action poses (such as firing and charging) and people in domestic poses (such as cooks, nurses and doctors),

LEFT Like most Heyde figures, the head of this Austrian infantryman with fixed bayonet plugs into the body. This solid figure stands just under 54mm (2¼in) high.

BELOW AND RIGHT While most lead 'flats' were made in Austria and Germany, these were probably made in Britain for inclusion in cigarette packets.

LEFT While the
Vatican Guard
(60mm/2¹/₄in
high) was made
by Figur of Italy,
the manufacturer
of the smaller
carabiniere and
Sturmabteilung is
unknown. All have
plug-in heads and
were made prior
to the Second
World War.

together with additions, such as encampments of tents and field hospitals, which increased the play-value for children. Mignot remained with conventional marching or ceremonial troops.

United Kingdom, America and the Soviet Union

German and French solid toy soldiers were exported to the United Kingdom and to America, and although some American manufacturers attempted to imitate the solid process in the late nineteenth century, they were largely unsuccessful. In the United Kingdom, W.Y. Carman, a founder member of the British Model Soldier Society, introduced a range of solid figures, many depicting the uniforms of British regiments from history. This short-lived venture, which started in the mid-1930s, did not continue after the Second World War.

The collapse of the Soviet Union brought to light a number of Russian soldier companies that use solid-cast method. The Anglo-Russian Toy Soldier Company and Insel are but two companies who are making huge efforts to break into the worldwide market.

BELOW This solid American Honor
Guard figure was an experiment by
Stadden to provide military miniature
figures painted as toys.

LEFT An unusual (circa 1930) example
in that the solid guardsman plugs into
the semi-round body of the horse. The
figure stands 60mm (2³/₈in) high.

ABOVE Made by Greewood and Ball in the
late 1960s, this figure of an officer reading
orders is solid and intricately-painted.

Connoisseur figures

Solid toy soldiers, made not as children's
toys, but as military miniatures, were
available after 1945 from exclusive
shops such as Hummel and Tradition
in central London.

RIGHT The tin-
plate base on this
1815 volunteer
earmarks this as a
Charles Stadden
1973 miniature.

In the main, they were the
standard 54mm (2¼in) size.
However, larger sizes were made, sometimes
in kit form, ready for the collector to

assemble and paint; they were designed for
adults who were interested in precise
uniform detail. The development of these
figures was the start of the distinction
between model soldiers produced for
adults as opposed to toy soldiers
made for children.

Two of the best-known manufacturers
producing these model soldiers between 1950
and 1970 were Charles Stadden and Rose
Miniatures. This area of collecting, which was

given the nickname of 'connoisseur figures', enabled the purchaser to buy intricate reproductions of regimental uniforms in the form of miniature figures.

The interest in connoisseur or military miniatures continued in France, where these items could be purchased in exclusive shops near the Musée de l'Armée, while New York's Madison Avenue and Polk's Hobby Stores provided the American collector with the opportunity to purchase military miniatures.

LEFT This mid-1960s Stadden solid 30mm (1¹/₄in) high model of Napoleon and his generals would have been sold through exclusive toy soldier shops.

BELOW Lacking in some refinement, these solid figures were most probably made in the Soviet Union in the late 1960s. They stand 52mm (2¹/₈in) high.

LEFT Made by Insel of Moscow, this hand-painted, solid figure (circa 1968) is 52mm (2¹/₈in) high.

The Swede Holger Eriksson designed the Authenticast toy soldier range that was manufactured in Ireland for the American company Comet. He also designed a set of 30mm (1¼in) troops for Swedish African Engineers, a company based in South Africa. These two companies provided the opportunity for collectors worldwide to obtain these solid, but expensive playthings. Figur of Italy and Alymer of Spain also manufactured similar items for the European market. Although connoisseur figures do not form a major part of the toy soldier collecting scene, they are interesting in that they were the first miniature soldiers to be made specifically for adult enthusiasts.

Hollow-cast figures

Until 1893, toy soldiers had been made of lead that was cast into solid figures. Although the process was expensive, it was the only one available. William Britain, a British toy manufacturer, had been producing

mechanical toys for several years before his son, William Britain Junior, conceived and perfected the hollow-cast method of production. This process was simple, but it revolutionized toy soldier production which had previously been dominated by solid figures.

The hollow-cast method enabled several figures to be cast from one quota of lead. Molten lead was poured into a cold mould that had an airhole and an escape route for any excess lead. The caster, with a deft movement of his wrist and great skill, swirled the molten metal around to coat the inside of the mould and poured out the excess. The extra lead could then be used again.

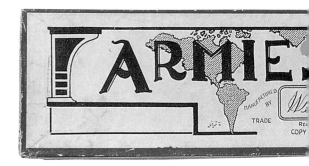

This method of production was much cheaper than previous techniques because it meant that several toy soldiers could be cast from the same amount of lead that would have produced only one solid soldier.

The finished soldier was, in fact, nothing more than a shell – empty and light. Quality controllers at the factory checked the weight, and overweight soldiers were put back into the melting-pot so that the lead could be reused. The figure was extracted from the mould with pliers before more lead was poured in to make another soldier. The cost of a hollow-cast toy was a fraction of that of a solid figure, needing only one-third of the quantity of lead.

Britains Ltd

The first set of hollow-cast figures produced by William Britain was a set of mounted Life Guards, which appeared in 1893 and was designated catalogue item No. 1. In keeping with the regiment's position within the British Army, item No. 2, which also appeared in 1893, was a set of Horse Guards. Both these sets contained five figures.

LEFT Crescent of Britain was a volume-producer of toy soldiers during the 1950s for the cheaper end of the market. They are of little value to collectors.

The first set of infantry figures (set No. 11) was also brought out in 1893. So began a long line of issues depicting regiments of the British Army.

The toy soldiers made by William Britain were an instant success, partly because of the lower cost and partly because of the attractive red boxes in which the soldiers were packaged. Colourful labels added to the attraction, and patriotic British families preferred to purchase a set of toy soldiers with 'Made In England' emblazoned on the box.

Britain approached Arthur Gamage, the owner of a large department store in Holborn, London, and persuaded him to purchase and feature only Britains soldiers in the store's Christmas displays. The subsequent marketing of Britains toy soldiers virtually brought an end to continental imports.

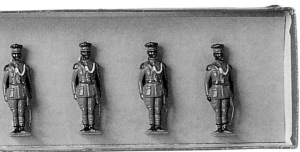

near to the Britains factory – A. Fry, C. D. Abel & Co. and Hanks Brothers, for example – and saw that the hollow-cast toy soldier was a money-spinner. Many of the employees or owners of these smaller companies had learned the hollow-casting method when they had been employed by Britains, and they decided to market their own versions of the hollow-cast figures. Many of these were flagrant copies of Britains toy soldiers, and in some cases, they were sold more cheaply than their competitor's products. Britains decided that it would have to stop this practice, and it carried out several successful prosecutions, forcing these smaller companies

Britains' production increased over the next few years. Arms were cast in individual moulds, thus making the arms movable, and the company's advertisements stressed this development and made the point that it increased the play-value for children.

ABOVE After being prosecuted for pirating Britains' designs, the companies Fry and Hanks Brothers did produce their own unique moulds.

In addition to British regiments, Britains produced regiments from other countries under the name of 'Armies of the World'. Production continued to increase up to and during the First World War.

Piracy and copyright

RIGHT One of Britains' more ambitious products (circa 1955).

The success of Britains toy soldiers brought problems. Many smaller manufacturers emerged just after the turn of the century in north London

BRITAINS MILITARY EQU

SELF PROPELLED 155m

A massive piece of Modern A used by the Major World Power

Ammunition and full instructions for firing

MANUFACTURED BY BRITAINS LTD., SUTHE
LONDON, E.17

LEFT A popular
and frequently-
found image in
Britains' 'Soldiers in
Action' range was
the infantry in
battledress. These
figures are 54mm
(2¼in) high.

to cease copying. Fry, Hanks and Abel, together with several others, regrouped, and came up with their own individual designs and continued in business.

This piracy taught Britains a valuable lesson, and the company started to apply copyright to its figures, at first using a paper sticker on the underside of the soldier's base, a method which began in 1900, and then, as the moulds wore out, having the trade name, date and copyright stamped on the bases of the figures or bellies of horses for mounted troops. The earlier paper stickers can help to date soldiers and also add to their value.

The Britains' factory assisted the war effort during 1914–18 by producing lead munitions components. This did not stop the production of toy soldiers, although it slowed down as the war progressed. The company had issued its first examples of khaki troops in 1899.

Britains established an office in Paris in 1905 and this resulted in the creation of new figures, many based on the uniforms of French units. Gun teams and ambulance wagons with troops in the khaki uniforms of the First World War were added in 1916. As uniforms changed leading up to 1938, Britains updated their models. As the British factory scaled down its production, the French office kept going. These issues are a rare find.

All change

After the First World War, horse-drawn vehicles, cowboys and Indians, boy scouts and artillery pieces were introduced to the range. Large quantities of sets representing famous regiments, both British and foreign, were produced up until 1938 when the factory

BELOW This
54mm (2¼in)
high cannon by
Britains has
cropped up
numerous times in
the range.

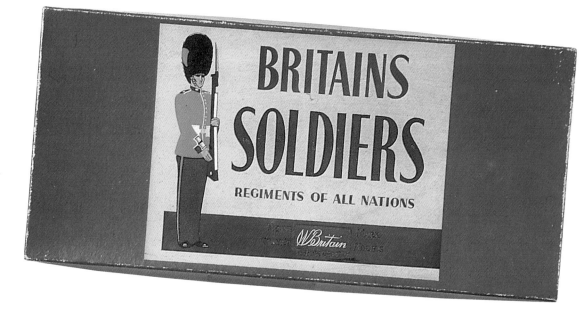

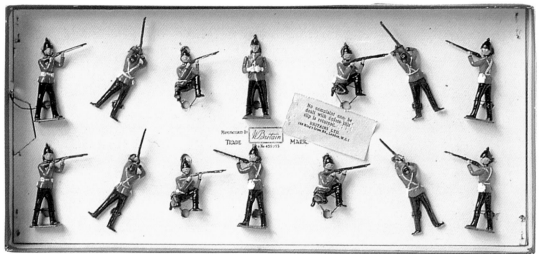

was turned over to munitions work. One of the final achievements prior to the war was the design and issue of the State Coach in time for the 1937 Coronation.

After the Second World War, government restrictions on the availability of lead proved to be frustrating.

Britains even went to the extent of advertising that it was ready to restart production, and it urged the buying public to write to their Members of Parliament to have government legislation relaxed to release lead for toy manufacture. The process was slow and at first only partially relaxed, so that toys could be made for export

LEFT A Britains'
box lid (circa
1954). The
'Historical Series'
included
Coronation issues
and Knights of
Agincourt figures.

RIGHT The action poses of these
Knights of Agincourt figures were a
welcome change from the static styles
that marked many of the 'Historical
Series'. This boxed set was designed for
Britains by Roy Selwyn Smith.

to bolster the ailing post-war economy. It was not until the late 1940s that home production recovered.

'Regiments of All Nations', which contained foreign, Commonwealth and Empire troops of the period was the name chosen to replace 'Armies of the World'.

Probably the most significant post-war event was the Coronation of Queen Elizabeth II. The State Coach was revived and footmen, grooms and Yeomen of the Guard were added, along with many new issues of units of the British and Empire forces that were to march in the Coronation Procession.

In 1954, Roy Selwyn Smith (previously with M. Zang at Herald) was employed as a designer and this resulted in a series of action figures entitled 'Knights of Agincourt'.

Toy soldiers in individual boxes and named 'Picture Packs' were issued in 1959. They were mainly taken

ABOVE This hollow-cast figure of an airman in donkey jacket was made by John Hill and Co. during the 1930s. Standing 54mm (2¹/₄in) high, it was one of a range sold in Woolworths.

ABOVE Collecting female military figures has become a specialized area. This hollow-cast nurse by John Hill and Co. was produced both before and after the Second World War.

from existing sets and just packaged separately, although a few new figures were designed to increase the range. These are rare and are now much sought after by collectors. The series lasted for six years. The design of some boxed sets changed shortly after this and cellophane windows appeared on the boxes.

Government regulations governing the lead content in children's toys were introduced in 1967, and Britains toy soldier production was scaled down to conform. In 1966 hollow-cast lead toy soldiers were deleted from Britains' catalogues.

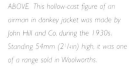

RIGHT In 1945, John Hill and Co. replaced the Royal Scots Grey standard bearer's lead flag with a paper one due to shortages. The figure is 90mm (3¹/₂in) high.

28

Other British firms

Since 1893, more than 100 British firms produced hollow-cast toy soldiers and figures. Before 1914 John Hill, Fry, Hanks, Reka and BMC were perhaps the most prolific. John Hill and Co. was Britains' main rival. The founder of the company, George Wood, had been an employee of Britains.

Wood designed his own unique range of soldiers, which some would say are on a par with Britains', though they appear more animated. Johillco's products proved

popular with children of working class families, who could identify the soldiers' poses with the military exploits of their fathers or brothers. Hill also issued ceremonial troops, airmen, cowboys and Indians and a vast range of other toy soldiers.

John Hill suffered two devastating blows. First, the factory was bombed during the London Blitz. The moulds somehow survived and were bought and taken to Burnley in Lancashire, where a consortium of businessmen set up a new factory.

The company had made no plans for the demise of hollow-cast figures, however, and its decision not to invest in plastic injection moulding technology dealt the company its second blow. It was forced into liquidation during the early 1960s.

Fry, Hanks and BMC had ceased trading before 1938; Crescent bought out Reka and continued to produce lead figures until 1959; and Charbens and Taylor & Barratt emerged in 1920. These manufacturers made the transition to plastic production.

A handful of new companies emerged after 1945, with Timpo (Toy Importers) being by far the most successful. With the assistance of Roy Selwyn Smith, Timpo produced some of the best hollow-cast toy soldiers to be made in post-war years – the company was active between 1946 and 1955.

LEFT AND BELOW Both from the barracks of John Hill and Co. is a mounted Field Marshall with baton (circa 1950s) and Highland Piper. The Piper was available in many tartans and the grade of paintwork determined its final price.

Beyond Britain

On the continent and in the USA, the hollow-cast method was adopted, but not to such an extent as in the United Kingdom. German manufacturers preferred to stick to solid-cast items, 'flats' or composition figures, rather than turn to hollow-cast production. French manufacturers adopted hollow-casting with more enthusiasm. And in the United States, the majority of so-called 'dimestore' figures were made by a hollow- or slush-cast method, but Edward Jones of Chicago used more conventional hollow-casting methods, relying on the firm of Sale in Birmingham, England to produce moulds for sale in the United States. Jones was a brilliant designer but a poor businessman. Although his figures are much sought after today, he did not achieve fame during his lifetime.

THIS PAGE Some 40 years separates these John Hill and Co. figures. The khaki charging figure with fixed bayonet was first made in the early 1900s, while the charging Highlander and kneeling guardsman herald from the 1950s. Some of these figures remained in production for many years.

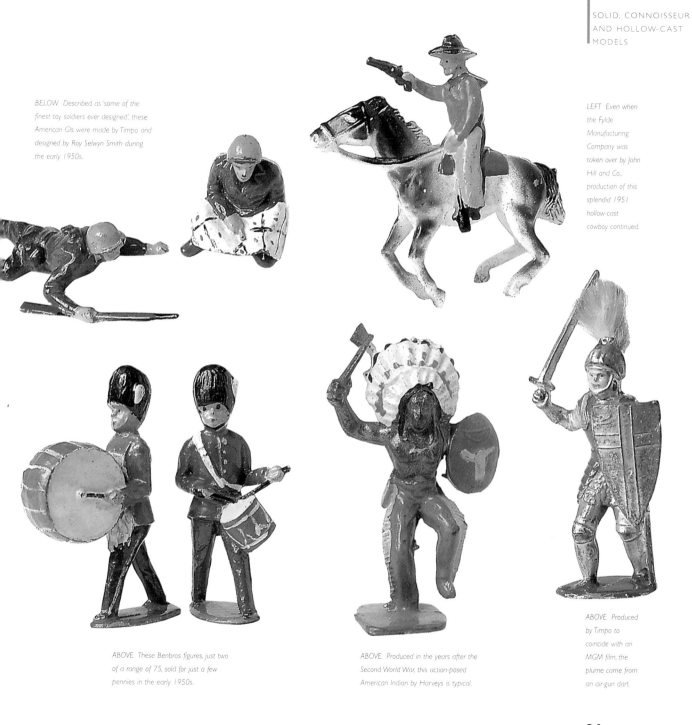

BELOW *Described as 'some of the finest toy soldiers ever designed', these American GIs were made by Timpo and designed by Roy Selwyn Smith during the early 1950s.*

LEFT *Even when the Fylde Manufacturing Company was taken over by John Hill and Co., production of this splendid 1951 hollow-cast cowboy continued.*

ABOVE *These Benbros figures, just two of a range of 75, sold for just a few pennies in the early 1950s.*

ABOVE *Produced in the years after the Second World War, this action-posed American Indian by Harveys is typical.*

ABOVE *Produced by Timpo to coincide with an MGM film, the plume came from an air-gun dart.*

LEFT A 54mm (2¹/₄in) high Greek
Evzone figure made by Edward Jones of
Chicago. Though his figures sold through
dimestores, this hollow-cast figure and
many others made by Jones are rare
and attract feverish bidding.

BELOW A French hollow-cast figure of
the 1950s made by GM. The captain at
his wheel stands 52mm (2¹/₈in) high.

BELOW Britains produced this
coronation coach in 1953, but the first
one appeared in 1937. Though many
thousands were made, an example like
this in its original box will command a
high price at auction. The figures are
54mm (2¹/₄in) high.

CHAPTER THREE

COMPOSITION AND SLUSH-CAST FIGURES

• • • •

Composition toy soldiers are made from a combination of materials, the commonest being a mixture of sawdust, glue, kaolin and casein. This mix was devised in Vienna in 1898 by a company named Pfeiffer. The mixture was shaped around a wire armature, left to dry and then hand-painted. The material was especially popular in Germany, and in 1926 Hausser, two brothers from Stuttgart, adopted the name Elastolin for their composition figures. This name is used today to refer to all composition figures, although strictly it should be used for Hausser items.

Elastolin

Elastolin was to used to produce 70mm (2¾in) figures from 1904 to 1943, although some of the early figures were as large as 100mm (4in). Most of the world's armed forces were portrayed in the Elastolin range, but during the 1930s, the range changed to reflect the German armed forces and the rise of the Nazi regime.

Elastolin's main competition came from Lincol in Dresden. Both manufacturers issued figures depicting German personalities, such as Hitler, Hess and Goering. These figures, which can command high prices, were often given porcelain heads to increase facial detail.

The Italian firm of Figur Brevitt made some Elastolin-type figures of Italian soldiers and Vatican guards but, with the exception of Durso (Belgium) and Durolin (Czechoslovakia), few other countries used composition for toy soldiers.

BELOW These bandsmen with their oval bases (circa 1930s) are typical of those produced by Hausser-Elastolin.

After the Second World War, while lead was still in short supply, the Brent Toy Company in England issued a small range of khaki infantry based on the Elastolin idea, using the name Elastolene, and the Timpo company introduced composition 'Timpolene' figures to its range.

Miller in the United States made some 100mm (4in) figures during the 1950s, using a plaster of Paris concoction, and in the United Kingdom, some large-size figures, more akin to statuettes, were issued by Riviere and Willett. However, these ventures were short lived – with the conventional lead toy soldier regaining the upper hand once restrictions on the use of lead were lifted by the government.

RIGHT Toydell made this Yeoman of the Guard in the mid-1950s, using plaster or composition material. It stands 100mm (4in) high.

RIGHT Most probably made by one of the Austrian or German companies, this composition nurse stands 65mm (2¹/₂in) high.

LEFT Standing 60mm (2³/₈in) high, this Vatican Guard was manufactured by the Italian company Figur Brevitt using a composition process devised in Austria.

LEFT A field-hospital nurse, standing
100mm (4in) high, is made of plaster
of Paris. Manufactured in the United
States by Millar, it was sold in 'five and
dime' stores.

BELOW Though more ornamental than
toy-like, this Indian Sikh (circa 1938) is
made of plaster. Few plaster figures
were made in the United States,
making this a rare example. It is
100mm (4in) high.

ABOVE Produced
in the United
Kingdom of
composition
materials, this
British infantryman
was sold through
Kresge stores in
the United States.
It stands 60mm
(2³/₈in) high.

ABOVE Millar's plaster of Paris figures,
like this stretcher party, are prone to
chipping, but still attract the attention of
a specialist group of collectors. The
figures stand 100mm (4in) high.

ABOVE This First World War
infantryman with standard is made of
composition material and was probably
produced by a French company. It
stands 70mm (2³/₄in) high.

35

Slush-cast and 'dimestore' soldiers

In the United States, toy soldiers were generally sold as individual figures rather than in boxed sets, and they were often stocked in the 'five and dime stores' (so called because they sold items costing five or ten cents). In the 1930s, toy soldiers produced in a similar way to British hollow-cast figures were sold in these stores, and they have come to be known as 'dimestore' figures, although a more accurate description would be slush-cast figures.

ABOVE Sold through dimestores, these American-made hollow-cast figures by Lincoln Logs resemble those made in the United Kingdom. The Mountie was part of a cowboys and Indians series, and the sailor from a standard military range.

The word 'dimestore' that is used to describe these soldiers was probably first used by collector and researcher Don Pielin. Without the research of Pielin and Richard O'Brien, who has written extensively on American 'dimestore' figures, the 'dimestore' figure may not have achieved the recognition it deserves.

ABOVE Nicknamed the 'correspondent', the soldier sits behind a wooden table. The genre of soldiers carrying out domestic duties is an interesting area of collecting.

Leading manufacturers

The best-known manufacturers of the 'dimestore' figures are probably the Barclay Manufacturing Company and Manoil, both of which began production

in the 1920s. In general, Manoil and Barclay figures are 70mm (2¾in) high, a size that is recognized as standard for American-made toy soldiers.

Grey Iron, a company that, as its name suggests, used a cast iron process, adopted the 'dimestore' size and style for its rather solid figures, as did Tommy Toy, All Nu. The Japanese-made 'Minikins' metal figures were also produced in standard sizes.

However, McLoughlin Jones, Lincoln Logs and Warren, other notable American makers, made toy soldiers more in keeping with the American size of 54mm (2¼in). Other soldiers retailed through dimestores and keenly collected in the United States include Auburn's rubber figures and Miller's plaster ones.

Barclay Manufacturing Company

Barclay, which was founded in 1924 by Donze and Michael Levy, operated in West Hoboken, New Jersey, and it grew to become the largest manufacturer of toy soldiers and figures in the United States. The nucleus of the company's production was devoted to models of American armed forces, mostly in action, and cowboys, Indians and other figures depicting the Wild West.

The khaki troops made before 1939 had removable tin helmets, although post-war figures had fixed helmets. After 1945 the figures' bases were removed and the feet widened so that each model was free-standing. This system, which was nicknamed 'podfoot', conserved lead. The company's output included pirates, knights, sailors, Japanese troops, motorcycle and sidecar combinations, parachutists and firemen, as well as civilian items depicting American social history.

The advent of plastic led to 'dimestore' production being phased out at the end of the 1950s. Barclay closed down in 1971.

Manoil

Maurice and Jack Manoil joined with Walter Baetz in 1924 to found the company that bears their name. It produced soldiers that were similar in scale and style to those made by Barclay, but perhaps with just an ounce more character. The Manoil 'Happy Farm' civilian range was produced to reflect social history and, like Barclay, Manoil produced a wide range of military vehicles.

Other American manufacturers

Grey Iron used the same 'dimestore' scale as Manoil and Barclay, but its figures were produced in cast iron. Home-cast toy soldiers were very popular in the 1930s. Casting sets containing metal moulds, a bar of lead, a ladle and a melting-pot

LEFT
A 'dimestore' naval ensign from Manoil, standing 75mm (3in) high. Similarities to a Barclay figure were inevitable considering the manufacturing process involved and the limited number of poses possible.

LEFT Dating from 1906, these figures were made by The American Soldier Company under the trade name Eureka. They stand 54mm (2¹/₄in) high.

37

became popular, in particular with children in remote areas, and could be ordered by mail. Sachs and Henry Schiercke were the best-known home-cast producers.

In the mid-1980s, Ron Eccles of Burlington, Iowa, who had acquired many of Barclay's and Manoil's original moulds, began to cast excellent copies of the 'dimestore' soldiers. Each item is marked 'Eccles Brothers' and dated.

Made in Japan

Japanese-made toy soldiers were also sold through the 'five and dime stores' and can, therefore, be classed as 'dimestore' figures. After 1945, many American companies imported lead, composition and celluloid toy soldiers from Japan, many of which were copies of American or European products. The quality of the items was variable – Minikins, for example, were made of lead and were of high quality, while Trico made crude composition figures.

Nevertheless, all were sold in vast numbers and have a strong following among today's collectors, with items in boxes marked 'Occupied Japan' being of particular value. Minikins were also exported to the United Kingdom and to France, where many were purchased by GIs stationed there.

*ABOVE
A wonderfully
inventive pose
equalled by skilful
design techniques
are exhibited in
this Manoil M88
parachute jumper.
The figure is
75mm (3in) high.*

*RIGHT Soldier
operating a
searchlight proved
so popular it was
issued seven times
by Barclay. It
stands 75mm
(3in) high.*

ABOVE Marked 'Made in Japan' on the base, this American Indian carrying a spear, which stands 54mm (2¼in) high, is unusual in that a pivot through the arms allows them to move.

LEFT Playwood Plastics made this composition soldier, who wears a gas mask and holds a flare gun. It is 75mm (3in) high.

CHAPTER FOUR

THE PLASTIC
BATTLEGROUND

• • • •

Although experiments into plastic as a commercial material for toy soldiers took place in the mid-1930s, it was not until the late 1940s that a viable product was produced. It is uncertain which manufacturer made the first plastic toy soldiers.

In America, Beton was certainly supplying dimestores with unpainted 60mm (2⅜in) figures of battledress troops just after the Second World War, while in England hard, brittle plastic soldiers and cowboys and Indians were offered for sale by Airfix in 1947. Malleable Mouldings of Deal, Kent, imported a range of hard plastic figures, designed by Holger Erilesson. Though superior to anything produced before 1947, the venture failed, probably because the figures were sophisticated and collectors were reluctant to change.

Process of manufacture

Plastic figures are made by the process of injection moulding, in which the raw material is forced through holes in the centre of a brass mould by a power-assisted injection machine. Some of the companies that had

issued hollow-cast figures had their moulds converted to fit the plastic injection moulding machines. Timpo, Cherilea and Crescent, which all began to produce plastic figures around 1955, adopted this procedure before designing new moulds.

BELOW The commercial manufacture of plastic figures was pioneered by Malleable Mouldings in the United Kingdom in the late 1940s. The mounted Roundhead and guardsman are rare examples of an unsuccessful venture.

Britain's plastic fantastic

The first British maker to issue plastic figures was Zang Products (later Herald) which produced some of the finest plastic toy soldiers ever made. Khaki battledress infantry, American Civil War soldiers, Foot Guards, Life Guards, Horse Guards, Highlanders, cowboys and Indians, Trojan warriors and an Indian Army Sikh appeared during the early 1950s, packed in attractive, colourful boxes or on display cards of four figures. In 1953, the trade name Herald was adopted and a logo of a medieval herald was embossed on the underside of each figure's base.

John Hill and Co. converted some of its hollow-cast moulds to plastic in the early 1950s, but investment in the change was minimal. Not even an order from Kelloggs to supply hundreds of thousands of figures to be put into cereal packages, convinced the Hill management that the future lay in plastic. John Hill and Co. ceased trading in the late 1950s.

ABOVE Originally produced by M Zang, this Herald Trojan Warrior, 54mm (2¹⁄₄in) high, was added to the Britains range that included a mounted general with standard.

ABOVE RIGHT AND RIGHT These American Civil War Union and Confederate figures have movable heads and arms, though they are not strictly part of Britains' 'Eyes Right' range. The standards are made of paper.

Britains goes plastic

Around 1953, Britains Ltd formed an association with Herald Miniatures, which eventually resulted in Britains taking over the Herald name and company. Britains continued to issue the bulk of its plastic soldiers under the Herald name, which remained part of the Britains trade name for its plastic figures until the late 1970s.

Britains' introduction of 'Swoppets' revolutionized the world of plastic figures. The

'Swoppet' range included cowboys, Indians and knights with interchangeable heads, bodies and legs, and even individual separate weapons.

In 1960, the company gave the ceremonial or full-dress type of toy soldier some Swoppet-type features. The range was called 'Eyes Right' and the heads and arms were movable.

The 'Swoppet' range was extended in 1962 by the introduction of battledress infantry. American Civil War foot figures had formed part of the Herald range from the early 1950s, but it took some 10 years for the mounted troops of a 'Swoppet' variety to join them. The old foot figures were phased out and replaced by a newly-designed set. Most of the existing ranges were extended, with siege weapons being added in 1967.

'Deetail' figures, which were plastic with a lead base, first appeared in 1971. The range initially consisted of American and German Second World War infantrymen. It is interesting to note that in the Deetail range, lead was again featuring in the production of toy soldiers. As New Metal Models have taken on an increasingly important role in the Britains range, the range of plastic figures has diminished.

Timpo and Mr Tooth

Timpo, whose lead figures had been of exceptional quality, relied at first on converting existing moulds. It produced King Arthur and the Knights of the Round Table, which could also be purchased, unpainted, in boxes marked 'Action Pack'. Timpo adopted a Swoppet-type system, and it introduced hundreds of different toy soldiers by means of the interchangeable method.

BELOW These plastic toy soldiers were produced in Turkey. Each stands 60mm (2³/₈in) high and they were purchased in an Istanbul bazaar in the late 1970s.

Knights and Roman soldiers complete with chariots, khaki-clad troops, paratroopers and Second World War Germans, cowboys and Indians, and Mexicans were all part of the range.

Norman Tooth, who had worked for Timpo and had designed many Timpo items, continued to come up with new ideas to bolster the toy soldier industry in the mid-1970s. He devised a remarkable machine that would convert, cut, paint and assemble a complete figure. This automatic process produced Timpo's last range in 1978 – a series of Vikings. Timpo ceased production in 1979.

Other British manufacturers

Cherilea, whose figures were 60mm (2⅜in) high, introduced many new ranges, including soldiers in battledress, paratroopers, Chinese and German soldiers, and 8th Army troops, complete with a figure of Field Marshal Montgomery. It also issued historical sets, including Roundheads, Cavaliers and medieval knights.

Lone Star made ceremonial troops, German Afrika Korps and naval figures in action, as well as the obligatory cowboys and Indians. Charbens repeated much of these subject areas, but also produced pirates, Cossacks and a bull-fighting set.

Crescent introduced a superb series of British First World War troops, and also produced knights, Robin Hood, cowboys and Indians and guardsmen, which were eventually obtainable in cereal packets.

The smaller companies, such as Trojan, Speedwell, VP, UNA, Benbros, Gemodels, Kentoys and Sacul, survived for a short while, and by the late 1970s, only Cavendish Miniatures of Windsor (still in production), Airfix, Timpo and Britains remained. By the end of the 1970s, however, with the exception of the Cavendish range and cheap imports from Hong Kong, Britains had the field almost to itself.

Old soldiers never die

A new aspect of plastic toy soldier production emerged in 1989, when Giles Brown of Dorset Soldiers purchased many of the former Cherilea plastic moulds and started to issue the unpainted figures in self-coloured plastic, for the customers to decorate themselves. Marlborough of Wales bought the old Charbens moulds in 1990 and started a similar business. Michael Ellis of Acton, London, and his company, Marksmen, is re-issuing the cult Marx figures.

LEFT This figure belongs to Timpo's 1970s Swoppet-style range. Made of plastic the cowboy (wearing a fringed Cheyenne-type jacket) has a movable head and waist. It is 54mm (2¹/₄in) high.

Stateside

In the United States, plastic toy soldiers were available from a number of companies – Beton, Lido and Ausley – but the market was dominated by Louis Man & Co. This famous toy company specialized in the production of large boxed sets, known as playsets, which included unpainted toy soldiers, buildings and accessories.

Painted Marx soldiers were available in the 'Warriors of the World' series. The company also issued 150mm (6in) high figures, in both hard and soft plastics. Marx eventually opened factories in Germany, Hong Kong and in the United Kingdom. Marx items have a cult status and are avidly collected.

BELOW Produced by Timpo, this plastic mounted Viking was one of the last pieces made using the machinery designed by RN Tooth. The Viking has a movable head and waist, and stands 90mm (3¹/₂in) high.

43

On the Continent

Apart from the Hong Kong companies, who almost without exception resorted to copying or pirating designs, the European continent was the main source of plastic figures.

Starlux of France used hard plastic to depict a wide range of French Napoleonic troops, Foreign Legionnaires and military school cadets. The figures

were realistically modelled in good action poses with a high level of detail on the paint finish. It also issued a second-grade series of toy soldiers which was aimed at the lower end of the market.

Elastolin, which had been famous before 1939 for its composition figures, was keen to supply the toy soldier market again. Unfortunately, occupying nations imposed restrictions on the production of 'war-like' toys. Elastolin did eventually manage to re-establish itself, but finally it fell victim to the new technology toys.

BELOW LEFT The Japanese flooded the world market with these plastic toy soldiers. Usually left in an unpainted state but well-detailed, they are regarded as second-class figures. This grey-plastic American infantryman is 80mm (3¹/₈in) high.

LEFT This cowboy with swag and gun has a movable waist. It is a Hong Kong copy of a Swoppet-style toy. It is 52mm (2¹/₈in) high.

LEFT A Hausser plastic Royal Canadian Mountie Policeman, 65mm (2¹/₂in) high, which was designed with the souvenir market in mind.

BELOW These are Michael Ellis Marksmen reproductions of Marx originals. Marx issued up to 100 self-coloured plastic figures in sets during the 1960s. These figures stand 60mm (2³/₈in) high.

BELOW This 60mm (2³/₄in) high figure of a Spanish Army standard bearer was made by Reamsa of Spain and was included in a set of 20 figures. Reamsa made plastic figures during the 1960s.

ABOVE These plastic figures are by Starlux and stand 54mm (2¹/₄in) high. The female Russian soldier is a departure from the normal subject, the jester is a first-grade range figure, and the paratrooper a second-grade figure.

RIGHT This rare figure of a toy-town soldier was made in plastic by Quiralux. The moulds were sold in the 1950s to Wend-Al who converted them for use with aluminium. These 'unbreakable' figures were a great success.

Spain's main producer was Reamsa, whose range of locally-inspired figures was popular from the 1950s to 1970s. The collector Ric Bracamontes, of Company B, Chicago, has reissued some Reamsa figures.

In Italy, the toy soldier market is, at the time of writing, dominated by Atlantic. The company has adapted its production methods and style to the Marx concept. Comansi, another Italian company, issues unpainted sets of Wild West items, as does Nardi, which includes American Civil War troops with movable waists.

CHAPTER FIVE

ALUMINIUM, PAPER AND WOOD FIGURES

• • • •

Miniature reproductions of soldiers can be found in all sorts of materials from ceramic and porcelain to glass, wood, resin, tin, celluloid and even soap. These items can vary tremendously in size, but do not fall within the realms of the collectable toy soldiers discussed in this book. This is perhaps because there is not a sufficient range of items available to fulfil a collector's needs. However, it is worth knowing a little about these 'curiosities' as you are bound come across them and they can be a pleasing addition to a collection.

Aluminium

Most of the aluminium figures were produced in France during the 1930s, although some were produced by the firm Wend-An in the United Kingdom a little later.

The method of production was developed by the French firm Quiralu just before the Second World War. A sand-based moulding tray in two halves was used to convert the aluminium into a toy soldier. The process resulted in a cruder casting than that of lead figures.

Aluminium soldiers were described as unbreakable and were certainly more resilient than their lead counterparts. The transitional period between lead and plastic gave the aluminium producers a sales opportunity. However, they never really became popular and were soon superseded by plastic models. Quiralu became Quiralux, and turned to plastic production, selling their moulds and rights to Wend-An, which used the trade name Wend-Al in the early 1950s.

Aluminium soldiers do not have the same amount of fine detail as lead soldiers owing to the softer-style casting procedure. Paint tends to chip more easily and the bases are thick, giving the figures a clumsy appearance. Although

BELOW Made of aluminium, this Robin Hood mounted on prancing horse was made by Krolyn of Copenhagen prior to 1939.

perhaps not part of the mainstream toy soldier hobby, there are small groups of collectors in France and Britain who are beginning to realize the potential of aluminium as a basis for a soldier collection. This growth in popularity is reflected in the prices being achieved by aluminium soldiers at auction.

Paper

Paper toy soldiers were made in the United States by Parker Brothers, Milton Bradley and McLoughlin, usually as part of shooting games. Paper or cardboard toy soldiers were fitted with a wooden block base so that the soldiers could be slotted into the base. These games were supplied with cannons or pop guns to enable the soldiers to be shot

ABOVE This tin-plate toy soldier, manufactured by Marx, was included in a pop-gun shooting game set. It stands 50mm (2in) high. Some enthusiasts have formed interesting collections around these tin-plate figures.

at. Understandably, many examples have not survived. These are not really major collectors' items as toy soldiers, but tend to form part of collections of children's games and toys.

Wood

Wooden soldiers are in existence – these are really toys – but wood was also an obvious choice for the construction of toy forts. Manufacturers of toy forts often co-operated with toy soldier manufacturers so that the forts would be the right scale for the soldiers and so on. Forts can be collectors' items in their own right, but they are bulky and require generous storage space. They complement a collection of toy soldiers very nicely.

BELOW Probably dating from 1920, this paper soldier, standing 100mm (4in) high, formed part of a shooting game. Similar figures were also made in cardboard.

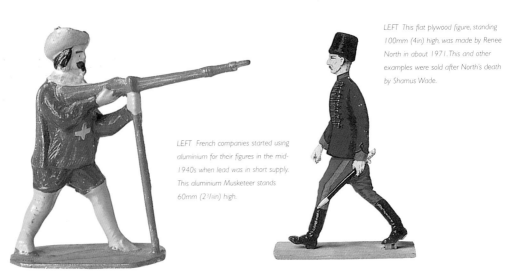

LEFT French companies started using aluminium for their figures in the mid-1940s when lead was in short supply. This aluminium Musketeer stands 60mm (2³/₈in) high.

LEFT This flat plywood figure, standing 100mm (4in) high, was made by Renee North in about 1971. This and other examples were sold after North's death by Shamus Wade.

A NEW ERA – TOY SOLDIERS SINCE 1973

• • • •

W hen the production of hollow-cast toy soldiers came to an end in 1966, plastic toy soldiers, solid military miniature items and discontinued hollow-cast figures were the only choices open to the toy soldier collector. However, the situation changed in 1973, when New Toy Soldiers burst on to the market almost simultaneously from two non-related sources.

New Toy Soldiers

Frank and Jan Scroby in the United Kingdom were perhaps the first to recognize that there was a demand for toy soldiers made in the style of the out-of-production hollow-cast figures. The Scrobys had been selling old hollow-cast figures from their stall on Portobello Road Market, London, but examples were becoming difficult to obtain.

They experimented with non-toxic, white metal substances and developed their own range of what are now known as 'New Toy Soldiers'. This all-embracing title is applied to all solid, white metal toy soldiers and figures designed, manufactured and painted in the style of, and complementary to, the old-style hollow-cast figures. It was indeed the original intention of the Scrobys that their newly-produced items would fit neatly into existing hollow-cast collections

Blenheim, the name of the street in which the Scrobys were living, was the name chosen to launch the range. It was an instant success with a collecting fraternity that had been starved of a traditional toy soldier for some seven years.

For the purist, the 'Blenheim' range raised a small problem in that the toy soldiers stepped off on the 'wrong' foot. But this was a minor irritation, which was quickly overlooked by collectors.

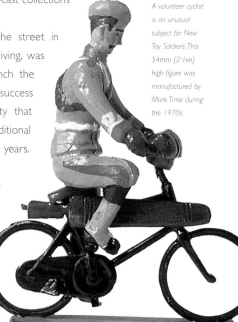

BELOW
A volunteer cyclist is an unusual subject for New Toy Soldiers. This 54mm (2¹⁄₄in) high figure was manufactured by Mark Time during the 1970s.

A touch of nostalgia

Shamus Wade, a long-established leader in the sale of old toy soldiers, was quick to recognize the potential of this new venture. He entered into an agreement with the Scrobys to produce for him an exclusive range, named 'Nostalgia', which would be sold by him through his mail order lists. The sets and individual figures were produced in limited numbers and were to depict units of regiments of the British Commonwealth.

The subject matter, although sometimes obscure, brought forth a unique range of New Toy Soldier regiments. During its latter years, the 'Nostalgia' range was taken over by Peter Cowan and Andrew Rose.

At the very time Frank and Jan Scroby were starting their venture in London, Britains Ltd also realized that the disappearance of the hollow-cast figures left a tremendous void. Britains' response was to issue a die-cast lead, marching Guardsman on a thick, green, die-cast base. The soldier's busby was plastic and the overall size was somewhat larger than the previous standard hollow-cast range.

The Scrobys' successful venture resulted in the emergence of many other New Toy Soldier manufacturers who produced their own ranges. Andrew Rose, a talented designer, has played a part in designing ranges for several companies, including his own range of Bastion and Wessex figures.

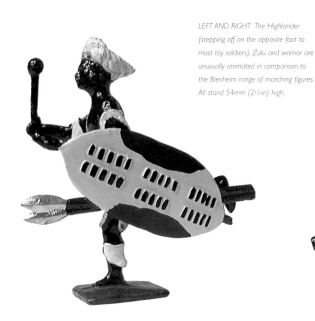

LEFT AND RIGHT The Highlander (stepping off on the opposite foot to most toy soldiers), Zulu and warrior are unusually animated in comparison to the Blenheim range of marching figures. All stand 54mm (2¹/₄in) high.

ABOVE Standing 54mm (2¼in) high,
this Chelsea Pensioner from the New
Toy Soldiers range is a colourful and
appropriate addition to parade scenes.

BELOW LEFT, BELOW AND BELOW
RIGHT Made by Trophy to fill a gap
left by the ending of hollow-cast were
these officers of the West India
Regiment, Indian Army and Royal
Marines. All are 54mm (2¼in) high.

ABOVE A young Sir Winston Churchill
firing a pistol at Dervisher is just one of
a range of superb miniatures produced
by Trophy Miniatures of Wales. Also in
the range are Rorke's Drift figures from
the Zulu War.

ABOVE This soldier from the Boxer
Rebellion was made by Blenheim for a
well-known collector in the 1970s. It
stands 54mm (2¼in) high.

In the mid to late 1970s, many manufacturers came and went – Gunner, Mark Time, British Bulldog, Albion, B.G. of G.B., Trafalgar, Militia, Jacklex, Empire, Campaign, M.J. Mode and Soldiers Soldiers, for example. Some have been revived or have merged under new ownership.

Of the major toy manufacturing companies, Trophy of Wales, which is run by Len Taylor, has become world famous for the quality of its design and painting. The Zulu War features heavily in the Trophy range.

Ducal of Hampshire is a company which specializes in figures to re-create ceremonial occasions, such as the Trooping the Colour at Buckingham Palace, and it will supply through its superb range enough toy soldiers to re-create any major procession.

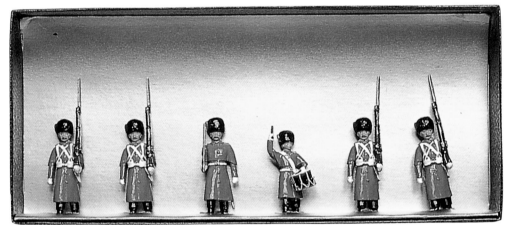

RIGHT An example of the blue and gold packaging used by Frank and Jane Scroby when they were producing the Blenheim models.

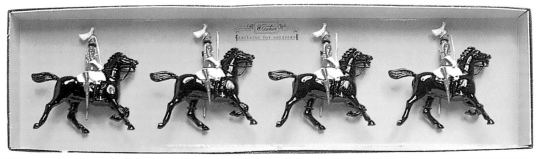

*LEFT AND
BELOW The New
Metal Model
version of a 1950s
hollow-cast Life
Guard was joined
in 1994 by a
boxed set
containing
examples of the
2nd Life Guards.
This release
marked the 101st
year of toy soldier
production. The
figures stand
100mm (3¹/₂in)
high.*

The Blenheim range ceased in 1982, but the Scrobys introduced a new range, 'Marlborough'. A magnificent series in the form of the Delhi Durbar of 1902 was introduced, which was devised so that the collector could add to the set and build up a complete Durbar.

Dorset Soldiers, owned by Giles Brown in Wiltshire, started in 1979. A wide range of United Kingdom and foreign regiments can be obtained, and new additions are added to the catalogue.

New toys Stateside

Among the best-known producers of New Toy Soldiers in America are Somerset, Bill Hocker, Edward Barley, Joe Shimek and Stephen Dietz.

RIGHT Boxed
inside a Perspex
case, these
Britains New
Metal Models of a
Yeoman of the
Guard, Scots
Guard and Horse
Guard are popular
souvenir items.

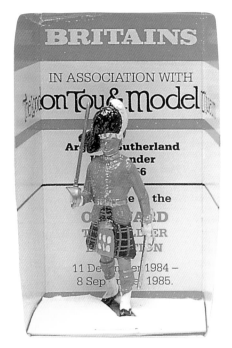

Perhaps the most famous range of New Toy Soldiers comes from William Hocker of California. His commitment, eye for detail and exquisite design and manufacturing techniques produce a world-famous product, which comes as close to old hollow-cast figures as possible. These, with many of the superb designs created by companies such as Trophy and Ducal, must be the toy soldier investments of the future.

New metal models

Britains' 'New Metal Models' arrived on the toy soldier scene in 1973, the same year as 'New Toy Soldiers', but they are quite different. Although they started at roughly the same time, 'New Toy Soldiers' established

RIGHT Two examples of short-issue figures released by Britains for an exhibition at the London Toy and Model Museum in 1984. These rare 54mm (2¼in) high figures were adapted from a standard Britains Highlander.

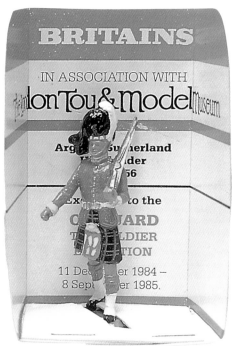

themselves much more quickly than did Britains' 'New Metal Models'. 'New Toy Soldiers' are made of white metal alloy, sculptured and produced from rubber moulds, usually by way of a centrifugal casting machine. The 'New Metal Models' require the manufacture of a metal die to facilitate the die-cast process. Britains' 'New Metal Models' are also slightly larger than the conventional 54mm (2¼in) toy soldier. This is in part due to the thick green metal base.

Britains has, since 1973, recaptured a large slice of the international toy soldier market. The initial issue of the Scots Guard marching figure in 1973 was the start of what has become a somewhat prolific range of figures. In 1974, two further individual items were produced by Britains to accompany the first Scots Guard. These new

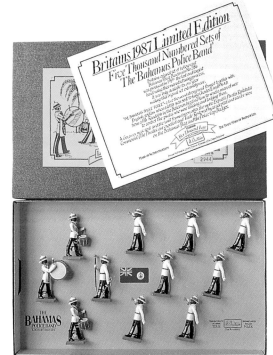

LEFT A numbered and limited set, complete with certificate, of the Bahamas Police Band. Britains had previously issued them in hollow-cast form. The figures are 54mm (2¼in) high.

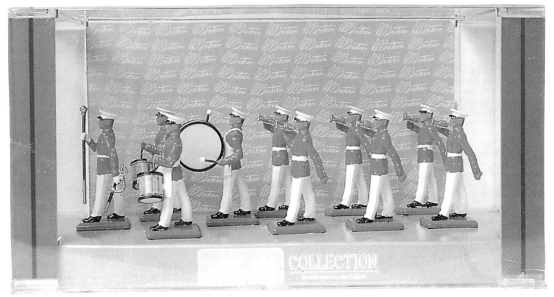

LEFT Standing 54mm (2¼in) high these Perspex-encased drummers and buglers of the United States Marine Corps are from the William Britain Collection.

The first of what became known as Britains Limited Editions was produced in 1983 and marketed in the United States through Reeves International. Set No. 5183, the Cameron Highlanders, consisted of eleven men and one officer in a red box, and included a certificate verifying its limited availability. The suffix on the set number indicated the year of issue to the collector. This set was exclusive to the United States,

LEFT Always a popular subject, this New Metal Model of a Royal Canadian Mounted Policeman stands 90mm (3¹/₂in) high. Britains has also issued versions in hollow-cast and plastic and in the Deetail range.

BELOW A William Britain limited edition set of the Royal Regiment of Fusiliers with regimental mascot. This particular set, as the card shows, was a prize to celebrate Britains' centenary year, 1993.

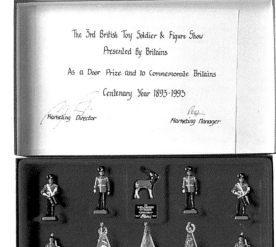

figures were a Yeoman of the Guard and a Life Guard, which were sold on backing cards. These popular figures were obviously an attempt to break into the London tourist market.

Three years later, six more figures were offered in cellophane-fronted boxes, but there then followed a curious period of inactivity by this successful company.

and its value has increased over ten times. Black Watch and Gordon Highlanders were introduced using a similar casting to that of the Cameron Highlanders. These sets were issued in picture-window boxes in unlimited quantities.

Mounted Life Guards and Horse Guards were brought out in 1984, again in cellophane-fronted window boxes. At the same time, the second limited edition set No. 5184 – this time for the home market and depicting Mounted Life Guards – was produced.

An exhibition at the London Toy and Model Museum entitled 'On Guard' prompted Britains to issue an officer and a man of the Argyle and Sutherland

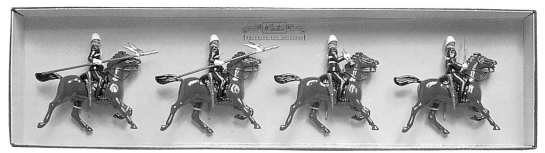

ABOVE AND LEFT Restoration of the traditional Britains' red boxes with illustrated descriptive labels happened in the 1990s. At the same time, Britains released toy soldiers in the style of the old hollow-cast figures.

57

BELOW *Britains produced special packaging for both Harrods and Hamleys, famous London stores. This Harrods London set shows HM The Queen dressed for Trooping the Colour, and a selection of troops.*

RIGHT *Intended for release in Britains' centenary year, this two-tier box with lift-out tray contains figures chosen by L.D. Britain. It was finally issued a year later. The figures stand 54mm (2¼in) and 90mm (3½in) high.*

Highlanders packed on an open-fronted card and available for the duration of the exhibition. Both are now much sought after by collectors.

From strength to strength

The investment potential of Britains limited edition sets varies according to the number of sets issued. The 1983 United States issue was limited to 3,000 sets. The first

window box. In 1986, the Household Cavalry range was extended further with the introduction of a farrier, standard bearer and trumpeters from both regiments. A London policeman was now included in the London souvenir sets.

The limited edition of 5,000 that appeared in 1986 was of the Welsh Guards with flags, and to enhance American sales, three sets of Marine Corps figures were also released. The Trooping the Colour ceremony came to life in a special set issued in 1987 in the form of a book, which opened to reveal the Queen and a representative array of the guardsmen who are present at the ceremony.

ABOVE This special, 1,000-edition commission from Britains Petite was requested in 1992 by the British Toy Retailers' Association.

United Kingdom issue in 1984 was of 7,000, and in 1985, 5,000 sets of the Seaforth Highlanders (set No. 5185) were released.

Her Majesty Queen Elizabeth II on horseback, in the uniform of Colonel-in-Chief as worn at the Trooping the Colour ceremony at Buckingham Palace each June in London, was released in 1985 in a cellophane-fronted

The same year also saw the introduction of a set of the Bahamas Police Band in a limited edition of 5,000. At the same time the 1986 Marine Corps range was extended to include bandsmen, guards, drummers and buglers.

The United States Marine Corps and guards regiments were further enhanced in 1988 by the introduction of colour parties. And a set of Royal Marines was also introduced on to the market, together with the Seaforth Highlanders wearing their tropical uniform, this time in a limited edition of 7,000 sets.

Repackaging and branding

A great deal of repackaging of existing ranges occurred in 1989, and the Middlesex Regiment was the only addition to the standard range. However, the company appears to have recognized the potential of the limited edition range, and two different limited sets were issued – the 22nd Cheshire Regiment and the Royal Marines in tropical dress, both sets restricted to 7,000 each.

Harrods and Hamleys, the famous London stores, negotiated with Britains to supply Britains soldiers in special boxes with the store's name embossed on them. Though not included in Britains catalogues, these sets will increase in value.

LEFT The drum and bugles, with escorts and standards of the Green Howards, are fitted into slots from which they can be easily removed and replaced. This style of Britains' packaging has become known as 'Grey boxes'.

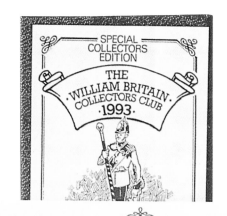

Britains, or Britains Petite, adopted William Britain as its sales name. The production of boxed sets continued to expand, the contents varying in 1991 to include the 17th Lancers and 21st Lancers, together with Irish Guards and Somerset Light Infantry.

Limited editions were also varied, the quantities different for each of three sets. The United States Army Band was intended as an exclusive Stateside release, but panic buying in the United Kingdom pushed the price up to astronomically high sums. However, many of the 5,000 sets were returned unsold from the United States, thus providing an excess and a fall in price. The Royal Welsh Fusiliers and the Honourable Artillery Company, in sets of 6,000 and 7,000 respectively, completed the year's releases.

In 1992, small boxes holding either one mounted figure or two foot figures were issued, signalling a partial return to the 1959 system used for the 'Picture Pack' series of hollow-cast toy soldiers. The limited editions were of the Royal Irish Rangers and the 9th/12th

Lancers, both in sets of 5,000, and the King's Own Border Regiment, in 6,000 sets. Five new sets in red boxes were introduced, including the Royal Marine Light Infantry and the Middlesex Yeomanry. A different style of packaging, grey boxes with lids, was used for ten figures, but this venture was short lived.

The Dennis Britain Set, the subject matter and content of which was chosen by the surviving member of the Britain family, was planned for release in 1992, but did not appear until 1993. It contained a selection of foot soldiers of fusilier regiments and hussars from cavalry regiments, in a two-tier box, designed to commemorate the centenary of the company.

The official centenary year was 1993, and three special sets were issued for sale only during the centenary year. There were the Royal Horse Artillery Gun Team, a Life Guard of 1837 and a Fort Henry Pioneer, each in individual boxes. Limited editions of 4,000 sets of the Royal Regiment of Fusiliers and 5,000 sets of the Band of the Blues and Royals, oddly enough without a bandmaster, were issued, along with the 5th Dragoon Guards and the King's Royal Rifle Corps, in red boxes.

RIGHT Issued in 1993, only 85 of these figures were produced as gifts. Each box is inscribed with the name of a person who attended a dinner celebrating Britains' centenary. The same year marked the 40th anniversary of HM The Queen's ascension to the throne.

COLLECTORS ITEMS FOR 14 YEARS UPWARDS

© BRITAINS PETITE LTD 1993 CHELSEA ST, NEW BASFORD, NOTTINGHAM NG7 7HR MADE IN ENGLAND

A LIMITED EDITION OF 85 PIECES COMMISSIONED FOR THE BRITAINS CENTENARY DINNER 26TH JUNE 1993

THE CORONATION OF
H.M. QUEEN ELIZABETH II
June 2nd 1953

THIS SET WAS PERSONALLY PRESENTED TO

Norman Joplin.

CAT No. 5891

CHAPTER SEVEN

SOUVENIRS
AND MEMORABILIA

● ● ● ●

The words 'toy soldier' at first conjure up the idea that they are simple playthings for children. As tastes change and toy soldiers of different materials have become antiques and collectables in their own right, they have come to appeal more to adults, and nostalgia or investment potential are important factors for the adults who collect them.

Toy soldiers sold as souvenirs in gift shops at airports, stately homes or tourist spots are, somewhat surprisingly, becoming collectable, and the Canadian market perhaps reflects this more than any other country in the world. The military-style uniform of the Royal Canadian Mounted Police is recognized by all who are interested in soldiers, and toy soldier manufacturers across the world have capitalized on the Canadian tourist market and produced figures of the famous 'Mountie' in all shapes and sizes and in various materials. Gift shops in the Niagara Falls area of Canada are crammed with examples of figures.

West Point Academy, New York, has also been a target of attention, with thousands of visitors each year

LEFT This guard dog is an example of a Christmas novelty from Dorset Soldiers. Produced in limited editions, the novelty characters combine military and comic subjects.

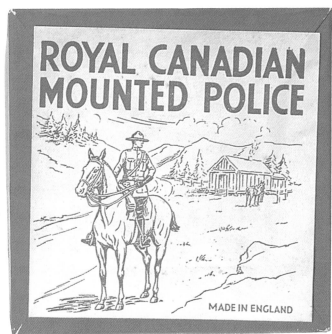

RIGHT This Crescent Royal Canadian Mountie is a rare, individually-boxed example produced for Canada's centennial in 1967. It was one of Crescent's last hollow-cast figures.

descending on the area; toy West Point Cadets are readily available. In Greece, the famous Evzone or Royal Guard with their unusual, colourful uniforms are an attractive proposition. Scotland, whose tourist industry must be one of the world's largest, is well supplied with Highlanders in all their regalia.

Toy shows also provide the toy soldier collector with a further chance to enhance a collection with souvenir badges or commemorative toy soldiers to bring back fond memories of an enjoyable day. This kind of merchandising is creating a new area of collecting, and sentimental collectors are now willing to pay inflated sums in order to acquire an item that celebrates a particular show.

RIGHT Collectors are taking souvenir figures seriously. This rocking horse, issued in limited numbers in 1992, is already a collectors' item. It stands 90mm (3¹/₂in) high.